For

WOMEN ON MEN

Compiled by
Lois L. Kaufman

Design by
Scharr Design

PETER PAUPER PRESS, INC.
WHITE PLAINS · NEW YORK

To the men in my life

Copyright © 1990
Peter Pauper Press, Inc.
202 Mamaroneck Avenue
White Plains, NY 10601
ISBN 0-88088-585-8
Library of Congress No. 89-63624
Printed in Hong Kong
5   4

Introduction

Women have always been eager to express their views about the opposite sex, and their attitudes about men transcend time and place, economic station, and nationality.

Women's comments about men are witty and irreverent, bawdy and discreet, loving and disdainful, but never—well hardly ever—passionless or distant.

Margaret Mead said, *Women want mediocre men, and men are working hard to be as mediocre as possible.* Mae West felt that if you *give a man a free hand he'll run it all over you.* And Gloria Steinem archly pointed out that *most men want their wives to have a jobette.*

Women on Men contains a full range of women's opinions on the opposite sex. Prepare to laugh, cry, fume—and get involved!

WOMEN ON MEN

Views on the Opposite Sex

Marrying a man is like buying something you've been admiring for a long time in a shop window. You may love it when you get it home, but it doesn't always go with everything else in the house.

JEAN KERR

Whenever I date a guy, I think, is this the man I want my children to spend their weekends with?

RITA RUDNER

One cannot be always laughing at a man without now and then stumbling on something witty.

JANE AUSTEN

Only one woman in ten recognizes her husband as the same man he was before she married him. Nine out of ten say he's changed. One in three says he's changed for the worse.

GALLUP SURVEY

I like to wake up feeling a new man.

JEAN HARLOW

Most men want their wives to have a jobette.

GLORIA STEINEM,
quoting a woman criminal lawyer

Time wounds all heels.

JANE ACE

Changing husbands is only changing troubles.

KATHLEEN NORRIS

Husbands are like fires. They go out if unattended.

ZSA ZSA GABOR

I will feel equality has arrived when we can elect to office women who are as incompetent as some of the men who are already there.

MAUREEN REAGAN

I married beneath me—all women do.

LADY NANCY ASTOR

No, I don't understand my husband's theory of relativity, but I know my husband and I know he can be trusted.

ELSA EINSTEIN

A woman's virtue is man's greatest invention.

CORNELIA OTIS SKINNER

Macho does not prove mucho.

ZSA ZSA GABOR

I'm for peace. I have yet to wake up in the morning and hear a man say, "I've just had a good war."

MAE WEST

It is sad and wrong to be so dependent for the life of my life on any human being as I am on you; but I cannot by any force of logic cure myself at this date, when it has become second nature. If I have to lead another life in any of the planets, I shall take precious good care not to hang myself round any man's neck, either as a locket or a millstone.

JANE CARLYLE

I think every woman's entitled to a middle husband she can forget.

ADELA ROGERS ST. JOHN

An archeologist is the best husband a woman can have; the older she gets, the more interested he is in her.

AGATHA CHRISTIE

The average man is more interested in a woman who is interested in him than he is in a woman—any woman—with beautiful legs.

MARLENE DIETRICH

Success has made failures of many men.

CINDY ADAMS

When an Italian talks with an American he's inclined to feel a twinge of inferiority. America is rich and strong, Italy is poor. But when he talks to me, he's more at ease. I still represent a big, strong nation but I am a woman and he's a man.

CLARE BOOTHE LUCE

My life didn't really begin until I met
Ronnie.

NANCY REAGAN

The success of any man with any woman is
apt to displease even his best friends.

ANNA LOUISE DE STAËL

Many Abolitionists have yet to learn the
ABC of woman's rights.

SUSAN B. ANTHONY

Latins are tenderly enthusiastic. In Brazil
they throw flowers at you. In Argentina they
throw themselves.

MARLENE DIETRICH

A lot of Johnny's problems stem from his relationship to his mother. I knew that woman really well. . . . She couldn't relate to her successful son.

> JOANNA CARSON,
> *ex-wife of Johnny Carson*

If love means never having to say you're sorry, then marriage means always having to say everything twice. Husbands, due to an unknown quirk of the universe, never hear you the first time.

> ESTELLE GETTY

I let Ike run the country and I ran the home.

> MAMIE EISENHOWER

Love will never be ideal until man recovers from the illusion that he can be just a little bit faithful or a little bit married.

> HELEN ROWLAND

All the men on my staff can type.

BELLA ABZUG

The great truth is that women actually like men, and men can never believe it.

ISABEL PATTERSON

No man can call himself liberal, or radical, or even a conservative advocate of fair play, if his work depends in any way on the unpaid or underpaid labor of women at home, or in the office.

GLORIA STEINEM

I never hated a man enough to give him his diamonds back.

ZSA ZSA GABOR

There will be some men who under no circumstances can allow a woman to pay a check. By all means, allow him to pay for his own outdated view of chivalry.

DEE WEDEMEYER

Woman must not depend upon the protection of man, but must be taught to protect herself.

SUSAN B. ANTHONY

Men look *at* themselves in mirrors. Women look *for* themselves.

ELISSA MELAMED

It takes a brave man to face a brave woman, and man's fear of woman's creative energy has never found an expression more clear than in the old German clamor, renewed by the Nazis, of "Kinder, Küche and Kirche" for women.

PEARL S. BUCK

When he's late for dinner, I know he's either having an affair or is lying dead in the street. I always hope it's the street.

JESSICA TANDY,
on her husband, Hume Cronyn

It is always incomprehensible to a man that a woman should refuse an offer of marriage.

JANE AUSTEN

Women want mediocre men, and men are working hard to be as mediocre as possible.

MARGARET MEAD

The man (Phil Donahue, her husband) does not know the meaning of the word *tidy*. He asked me one day, "Where are my shoes?" So I asked him, "Where are *my* shoes?" I don't know what it is about men. They think that women have radar attached to our uteruses.

MARLO THOMAS

Women's liberation is just a lot of foolishness. It's men who are discriminated against. They can't bear children. And no one's likely to do anything about that.

GOLDA MEIR

There is more difference within the sexes than between them.

IVY COMPTON-BURNETT

Do not put such unlimited power into the hands of the husbands. Remember all men would be tyrants if they could. If particular care and attention is not paid to the ladies we are determined to foment a rebellion, and will not hold ourselves bound by any laws in which we have no voice, or representation.

ABIGAIL ADAMS

A husband is what is left of the lover after the nerve has been extracted.

HELEN ROWLAND

If it's a woman, it's caustic; if it's a man, it's authoritative. If it's a woman, it's too often pushy; if it's a man it's aggressive in the best sense of the word.

BARBARA WALTERS

In passing, also, I would like to say that the first time Adam had a chance he laid the blame on women.

LADY NANCY ASTOR

If one could be friendly with women, what a pleasure—the relationship so secret and private compared with relations with men.

VIRGINIA WOOLF

Before marriage, a man will lie awake all night thinking about something you said; after marriage, he'll fall asleep before you finish saying it.

HELEN ROWLAND

16

If men could become pregnant, abortion
would be a sacrament.

FLO KENNEDY

The intelligent man who is proud of his
intelligence is like the condemned man who
is proud of his large cell.

SIMONE WEIL

If you want to sacrifice the admiration of
many men for the criticism of one, go ahead,
get married.

KATHARINE HOUGHTON HEPBURN,
mother of the actress

Men are creatures with two legs and eight
hands.

JAYNE MANSFIELD

Dr. Kissinger was surprised that I knew
where Ghana was.

SHIRLEY TEMPLE BLACK

Men weren't really the enemy—they were fellow victims suffering from an outmoded masculine mystique that made them feel unnecessarily inadequate when there were no bears to kill.

BETTY FRIEDAN

Don't accept rides from strange men, and remember that all men are strange as hell.

ROBIN MORGAN

I like men to behave like men. I like them strong and childish.

FRANÇOISE SAGAN

I react against the plain, the one-dimensional men. . . . I meet them everywhere, prosaic, down-to-earth, always talking of politics, never for one moment in the world of music or pleasure, never free of the weight of daily problems, never joyous, never elated, made of either concrete and steel or like work horses, indifferent to their bodies, obsessed with power.

ANAÏS NIN

I have known many single men I should
have liked in my life (if it had suited them)
for a husband; but very few husbands have I
ever wished was mine.

MARY LAMB

Beware of the man who praises women's
liberation; he is about to quit his job.

ERICA JONG

This has always been a man's world, and
none of the reasons hitherto brought
forward in explanation of this fact has
seemed adequate.

SIMONE DE BEAUVOIR

I refuse to consign the whole male sex to the
nursery. I insist on believing that some men
are my equals.

BRIGID BROPHY

[If men could menstruate] sanitary supplies would be federally funded and free. Of course, some men would still pay for the prestige of such commercial brands as Paul Newman Tampons, Muhammad Ali's Rope-a-Dope Pads, John Wayne Maxi Pads, and Joe Namath Jock Shields—"For Those Light Bachelor Days."

GLORIA STEINEM

When a girl marries she exchanges the attentions of many men for the inattention of one.

HELEN ROWLAND

If you want anything said, ask a man. If you want anything done, ask a woman.

MARGARET THATCHER

Deliver me from your cold phlegmatic preachers, politicians, friends, lovers and husbands.

ABIGAIL ADAMS

Men believe men are central to women's lives, and they're not—even when they become economically central, even psychologically, when we have to please them. Children are the center of a woman's life. Work is always central. When you have children, they become your work, your opus.

MARILYN FRENCH

All I ask our brethren is that they will take their feet from off our necks and permit us to stand upright.

SARAH GRIMKÉ

The man I don't like doesn't exist.

MAE WEST

. . . not one man, in the million, . . . no, not in the hundred million, can rise above the belief that Woman was made for *Man,* . . .

MARGARET FULLER

Our fathers waged a bloody conflict with England, because *they* were taxed without being represented . . . *They* were not willing to be governed by laws which *they* had no voice in making: but this is the way in which women are governed in this Republic.

ANGELINA GRIMKÉ

I love men, not because they are men, but because they are not women.

CHRISTINA, QUEEN OF SWEDEN

. . . it wasn't a woman who betrayed Jesus with a kiss.

CATHERINE CARSWELL

Summer bachelors, like summer breezes, are never as cool as they pretend to be. . . . There are plenty of men who philander during the summer, to be sure, but they are usually the same lot who philander during the winter—albeit with less convenience.

NORA EPHRON

Rex is the only man in the world who would disdainfully send back the wine in his own home.

ELIZABETH HARRISON,
on her husband, Rex Harrison

We will have equality when a female schlemiel moves ahead as fast as a male schlemiel.

ESTELLE RAMEY

Behind every great man there is a surprised woman.

MARYON PEARSON

Women have changed in their relationship to men, but men stand pat just where Adam did when it comes to dealing with women.

DOROTHY DIX

I require three things in a man: he must be handsome, ruthless, and stupid.

DOROTHY PARKER

If men can run the world, why can't they stop wearing neckties? How intelligent is it to start the day by tying a little noose around your neck?

LINDA ELLERBEE

A woman is a woman until the day she dies, but a man's a man only as long as he can.

MOMS MABLEY

Women have served all these centuries as looking-glasses possessing the magic and delicious power of reflecting the figure of man at twice its natural size.

VIRGINIA WOOLF

A bachelor never quite gets over the idea that he is a thing of beauty and a boy forever.

HELEN ROWLAND

Sexiness wears thin after a while and beauty fades, but to be married to a man who makes you laugh every day, ah, now that's a real treat!

JOANNE WOODWARD

Boys don't make passes at female smart-asses.

LETTY COTTIN POGREBIN

'Tis the established custom [in 1716 Vienna] for every lady to have two husbands, one that bears the name, and another that performs the duties.

MARY WORTLEY MONTAGU

It is a marvelous thing to be physically a woman if only to know the marvels of a man.

MARYA MANNES

The best way to hold a man is in your arms.

MAE WEST

If ever two were one, then surely we,
If ever man were loved by wife, then thee;
If ever wife was happy in a man,
Compare with me ye women if you can.

ANNE BRADSTREET,
To My Dear and Loving Husband

I never loved a man I liked—and never liked a man I loved.

FANNY BRICE

Women are not forgiven for aging. Bob Redford's lines of distinction are my old-age wrinkles.

JANE FONDA

He says his lust is in his heart. I hope it's a little lower.

SHIRLEY MACLAINE,
about Jimmy Carter

Jimmy's not sexy, he's my son.

LILLIAN CARTER

Very few people that have settled entirely in the country, but have grown at length weary of one another. The lady's conversation generally falls into a thousand impertinent effects of idleness; and the gentleman falls in love with his dogs and his horses, and out of love with everything else.

MARY WORTLEY MONTAGU,
1712

I can't think of any other time that a women's issue has so affected politics. It has suddenly become clear that someone who does not respect women is not fit to be Prime Minister of Japan.

KII NAKAMURA,
vice president of the Japan Housewives Association

Trust your husband, adore your husband, and get as much as you can in your own name.

Advice to Joan Rivers from her mother

If a man watches three football games in a row, he should be declared legally dead.

ERMA BOMBECK

But my biggest problem all my life was men. I never met one yet who could compete with the image the public made out of Bette Davis.

BETTE DAVIS

Man represents us, legislates for us, and now holds himself accountable for us! How kind in him, and what a weight is lifted from us! We shall no longer be answerable to the laws of God or man, no longer be subject to punishment for breaking them, no longer be responsible for any of our doings.

AMELIA JENKS BLOOMER

Gentlemen always seem to remember blondes.

ANITA LOOS

It is possible that blondes also prefer gentlemen.

MAMIE VAN DOREN

Gentlemen don't prefer blondes. If I were writing that book today, I'd call it "Gentlemen Prefer Gentlemen."

ANITA LOOS

As long as you know that most men are like children you know everything.

COCO CHANEL

Men control the political scene—internationally as well as nationally. They make the wars, and make the treaties. They control international finance. They make and interpret most of the laws, many of them disadvantageous to women, poor people, blacks, American Indians, Puerto Ricans, etc. While there are outstanding exceptions in the case of individuals, the male domination in many areas has been singularly insensitive to the needs of the weak.

CORETTA SCOTT KING

I think that implicit in the women's movement is the idea that women will share in the economic burden, and men will share more equally in the home and the family.

BETTY FRIEDAN

33

What is most beautiful in virile men is
something feminine; what is most beautiful
in feminine women is something masculine.
SUSAN SONTAG

Women have one great advantage over men.
It is commonly thought that if they marry
they have done enough, and need career no
further. If a man marries, on the other hand,
public opinion is all against him if he takes
this view.

ROSE MACAULAY

I only like two kinds of men: domestic and
imported.

MAE WEST

When Harvard men say they have graduated
from Radcliffe, then we've made it.

JACQUELINE KENNEDY ONASSIS

I never married because I have three pets at home that answer the same purpose as a husband. I have a dog that growls every morning, a parrot that swears all afternoon, and a cat that comes home late at night.

MARIE CORELLI

The fact is that men need women more than women need men; and so, aware of this fact, man has sought to keep woman dependent upon him economically as the only method open to him of making himself necessary to her.

ELIZABETH GOULD DAVIS

A woman without a man is like a fish without a bicycle.

GLORIA STEINEM

I don't like good-looking men—one always thinks they'll be dumb.

ALICE ADAMS

I just owe almost everything to my father
[and] it's passionately interesting for me that
the things that I learned in a small town, in a
very modest home, are just the things that I
believe have won the election.

MARGARET THATCHER

Abraham Lincoln immortalized himself by
the emancipation of four million Southern
slaves. Speaking for my suffrage coadjutors,
we now desire that you, Mr. President, who
are already celebrated for so many noble
deeds and honourable utterances, immortalize
yourself by bringing about the complete
emancipation of thirty-six million women.

ELIZABETH CADY STANTON

Probably the only place where a man can
feel really secure is in a maximum security
prison, except for the imminent threat of
release.

GERMAINE GREER

Our sex's weakness you expose and blame
Of every prating fop the common theme;
Yet from this weakness you suppose is due
Sublimer virtue than your Cato knew.
From whence is this unjust distinction
   shown?
Are we not formed with passions like your
   own?
Nature with equal fire our souls endued;
Our minds as lofty, and as warm our blood.

MARY WORTLEY MONTAGU,
1759

He has a future and I have a past, so we
should be all right.

JENNIE CHURCHILL,
*on her marriage to Montagu Porch,
a man younger than her son*

Oh my son's my son till he gets him a wife,
But my daughter's my daughter all her life.

DINAH MARIA MULOCK CRAIK

A bachelor has to have an inspiration for
making love to a woman—a married man
needs only an excuse.

HELEN ROWLAND

[Boxing is] a celebration of the lost religion of masculinity all the more trenchant for its being lost.

JOYCE CAROL OATES

The male sex, as a sex, does not universally appeal to me. I find the men today less manly; but a woman of my age is not in a position to know exactly how manly they are.

KATHARINE HEPBURN

We seem to have a great nostalgia for the good old days—"when men were men"—or so we think. I think we have greatly romanticized this picture. It was so much easier for a man to *look* masculine when women were subservient. A man didn't have to be a real man at all, and he could fool everybody, including himself. . . . He played a role, and no one ever really knew or thought about what he was or felt beneath the surface of that role.

EDA LE SHAN

If a man fights his adversaries, he's called determined. If a woman does it, she's frustrated.

ESTHER PETERSON

If you are looking for a kindly, well-to-do older gentleman who is no longer interested in sex, take out an ad in *The Wall Street Journal.*

ABIGAIL VAN BUREN

The history of men's opposition to women's emancipation is more interesting perhaps than the story of that emancipation itself.

VIRGINIA WOOLF

A broken heart is what makes life so wonderful five years later, when you see the guy in an elevator and he is fat and smoking a cigar and saying long-time-no-see. If he hadn't broken your heart, you couldn't have that glorious feeling of relief!

PHYLLIS BATTELLE

To a woman the first kiss is just the end of the beginning but to a man it is the beginning of the end.

HELEN ROWLAND

My husband is German; every night I get dressed up like Poland and he invades me.

BETTE MIDLER

Men of sense in all ages abhor those customs which treat us only as the vassals of your sex.

ABIGAIL ADAMS

No man is a hero to his valet.

MADAME DE CORNUEL

If woman had no existence save in the fiction written by men, one would imagine her a person of the utmost importance; very various; heroic and mean; splendid and sordid; infinitely beautiful and hideous in the extreme; as great as a man, some think even better.

VIRGINIA WOOLF

I don't mind being a grandmother, but I object to going to bed with a grandfather.

ANONYMOUS

Love is the history of a woman's life; it is only an episode in man's.

ANNA LOUISE DE STAËL

The average secretary in the U.S. is better educated than the average boss.

GLORIA STEINEM

Women are systematically degraded by receiving the trivial attentions which men think it manly to pay to the sex, when, in fact, men are insultingly supporting their own superiority.

MARY WOLLSTONECRAFT

Men define intelligence, men define usefulness, men tell us what is beautiful, men even tell us what is womanly.

SALLY KEMPTON

Where young boys plan for what they will achieve and attain, young girls plan for whom they will achieve and attain.

CHARLOTTE PERKINS GILMAN

Give a man a free hand and he'll run it all over you.

MAE WEST

The best thing a woman can do is to marry. It appears to me that even quarrels with one's husband are preferable to the ennui of a solitary existence.

ELIZABETH PATTERSON BONAPARTE, *1807*

Man reaches the highest point of lovableness at 12 to 17—to get it back, in a second flowering, at the age of 70 to 90.

ISAK DINESEN

I'm the most liberated woman in the world. Any woman can be liberated if she wants to be. First, she has to convince her husband.

MARTHA MITCHELL

A man in love is incomplete until he has married. Then he's finished.

ZSA ZSA GABOR

Women are being considered as candidates
for Vice President of the United States
because it is the worst job in America. It's
amazing that men will take it. A job with real
power is First Lady. I'd be willing to run for
that. As far as the men who are running for
President are concerned, they aren't people I
would date.

NORA EPHRON

A successful man is one who makes more
money than his wife can spend. A successful
woman is one who can find such a man.

LANA TURNER

The trouble with some women is that they
get all excited about nothing—and then
marry him.

CHER

A man's home may seem to be his castle on
the outside; inside, it is more often his
nursery.

CLARE BOOTHE LUCE

Whatever women do they must do twice as
well as men to be thought half as good.
Luckily, this is not difficult.

CHARLOTTE WHITTON

I do not believe that women are better than
men. We have not wrecked railroads, nor
corrupted legislatures, nor done many
unholy things that men have done; but then
we must remember that we have not had the
chance.

JANE ADDAMS

One reason we lasted so long is that we
usually played two people who were very
much in love. As we were realistic actors, we
became those two people. So we had a
divertissement: I had an affair with him, and
he with me.

LYNN FONTANNE,
*on 55 years of marriage
to Alfred Lunt*

46

Generally women are better than men—they have more character. I prefer men for some things, obviously, but women have a greater sense of honor and are more willing to take a chance with their lives. They are more open and decent in their relationship with a man. Men run all the time. I don't know how they live with themselves, they are so preoccupied with being studs.

LAUREN BACALL

A man is *so* in the way in the house.

ELIZABETH CLEGHORN GASKELL

Some men are so macho they'll get you pregnant just to kill a rabbit.

MAUREEN MURPHY

When men reach their sixties and retire, they go to pieces. Women just go right on cooking.

GAIL SHEEHY

Mad, bad, and dangerous to know.
                                    LADY CAROLINE LAMB,
                                        of Byron

Women speak because they wish to speak,
whereas a man speaks only when driven to
speech by something outside himself—like,
for instance, he can't find any clean socks.
                                        JEAN KERR

In his dealings with women the American
husband is, after all, only an amateur. The
gigolo is a professional. Whenever an
amateur and a professional compete in any
line of endeavor the professional is almost
without exception the victor.
                                    HELEN LAWRENSON

There is so little difference between
husbands you might as well keep the first.
                                    ADELA ROGERS ST. JOHN

A man may brave opinion; a woman must submit to it.

ANNA LOUISE DE STAËL

Implicitly adopting the male life as the norm, they have tried to fashion women out of a masculine cloth. It all goes back, of course, to Adam and Eve—a story which shows among other things that if you make a woman out of a man, you are bound to get into trouble. In the life cycle, as in the garden of Eden, woman has been the deviant.

CAROL GILLIGAN

It is not in giving life but in risking life that man is raised above the animal; that is why superiority has been accorded in humanity not to the sex that brings forth but to that which kills.

SIMONE DE BEAUVOIR

He was like the cock who thought the sun had risen to hear him crow.

GEORGE ELIOT

The core problem women face in combining career and marriage is, quite simply, their husbands. Their husbands' attitudes. Expectations. Fears. Insecurities.

DR. JOYCE BROTHERS

The usual masculine disillusionment in discovering that a woman has a brain.

MARGARET MITCHELL,
Gone With the Wind

The people I'm furious with are the women's liberationists. They keep getting up on soapboxes and proclaiming women are brighter than men. That's true, but it should be kept quiet or it ruins the whole racket.

ANITA LOOS

Man forgives woman anything save the wit to outwit him.

MINNA ANTRIM

The male has been taught that he is superior to women in nearly every way, and this is reinforced by the submissive tactics of many women in their desperate antics of flirtation and hunting; it would be a wonder if the average male did not come to believe that he was superior.

JOYCE CAROL OATES

The young men of today seem mostly to be interested in the manner rather than the matter.

ALICE B. TOKLAS

Fighting is essentially a masculine idea; a woman's weapon is her tongue.

HERMIONE GINGOLD

Whatever the rest of the world thinks of the English gentleman, the English lady regards him apprehensively as something between God and a goat and equally formidable on both scores.

MARGARET HALSEY

52

Men say they love independence in a woman, but they don't waste a second demolishing it brick by brick.

CANDICE BERGEN

If you never want to see a man again, say, "I love you, I want to marry you. I want to have children"—they leave skid marks.

RITA RUDNER

The academy has fought stoically to claim that *they* named the Oscar. But of course I did. I named it after the rear end of my husband. Why? Because that's what it looked like.

BETTE DAVIS,
on her first husband,
Harmon Oscar Nelson, Jr.

The same energy of character which renders a man a daring villain would have rendered him useful to society, had that society been well organized.

MARY WOLLSTONECRAFT

I like a man who can cry. My father cried.
My brother Rusty cries.

JESSAMYN WEST

I wouldn't trust my husband with a young
woman for five minutes, and he's been dead
for 25 years.

BRENDAN BEHAN'S MOTHER

I wouldn't have wanted to be an upstairs or
a downstairs woman. I would have wanted
to be a man. The women weren't allowed to
do anything.

JEAN MARSH,
of TV program Upstairs, Downstairs

The fantasy of every Australian man is to
have two women—one cleaning and the
other dusting.

MAUREEN MURPHY

It was never in my heart to slight any man,
but only that man should be kept in his
place and not sit in the room of God.

ANNE HUTCHINSON

God made man, and then said I can do
better than that and made woman.

ADELA ROGERS ST. JOHN

I would even go to Washington, which is
saying something for me, just to glimpse Jane
Q. Public being sworn in as the first female
president of the United States, while her
husband holds the Bible and wears a silly
pillbox hat and matching coat.

ANNA QUINDLEN

I'm not denyin' the women are foolish: God
Almighty made 'em to match the men.

GEORGE ELIOT

I'd like to get married because I like the idea of a man being required by law to sleep with me every night.

CARRIE SNOW

Sometimes I think all that terrific male equipment just hangs there by a thread.

LINDA LAVIN,
as character in movie
See You in the Morning

I'll have to have a room of my own. Nobody could sleep with Dick. He wakes up during the night, switches on the lights, speaks into his tape recorder.

PAT NIXON

Philip Roth is a good writer, but I wouldn't want to shake hands with him.

JACQUELINE SUSANN,
after reading Portnoy's Complaint

Men, the very best of men, can only suffer, while women can endure.

DINAH MARIA MULOCK CRAIK

Errol Flynn died on a 70-foot boat with a 17-year-old girl. Walter has always wanted to go that way, but he's going to settle for a 17-footer with a 70-year-old.

BETSY CRONKITE,
wife of Walter Cronkite

One-third mush and two-thirds Eleanor.

ALICE ROOSEVELT LONGWORTH,
on Franklin D. Roosevelt

Bill likes the way I do his shirts.

CONNIE CHUNG,
(on Bill Small, CBS News VP),
when asked how she had
advanced so far

My father taught me that comedy is mightier than the sword and the pen. And even though he was a sexist pig in every way, if I would say something that was very anti-male, or anti-him, and it was funny, my father would applaud and say, "Good one."

ROSEANNE BARR

If men were really what they profess to be they would not compel women to dress so that the facilities for vice would always be so easy.

MARY WALKER

If I don't feel like wearing a bra I don't wear one. I'd never let my nipples show at a state function, though—I'd be frightened the old men would have heart attacks.

MARGARET TRUDEAU

A man in the house is worth two in the street.

MAE WEST

Now, we are becoming the men we wanted to marry. Once women were trained to marry a doctor, not be one.

GLORIA STEINEM

Years ago, during a wave of crimes against women in Israel, a council of men asked Golda Meir to put a nighttime curfew on females. Meir said no. If men were the problem, she answered, let the council enforce a curfew against men.

ELLEN GOODMAN

Congress is a middle-aged, middle-class, white male power structure. . . . No wonder it's been so totally unresponsive to the needs of this country.

BELLA ABZUG

Men are more conventional than women and much slower to change their ideas.

KATHLEEN NORRIS

If you kept seeing Robert Redford stark naked on the screen, would he be a superstar today? No way. Or Gene Hackman showing everything? Their million dollar days would be over. I want to be in a movie where all the men take their clothes off and I don't.

CYBILL SHEPHERD

I asked a man in prison once how he happened to be there and he said he had stolen a pair of shoes. I told him if he had stolen a railroad he would be a United States Senator.

"MOTHER" MARY JONES

I hate mankind with all the fury of an old maid. Indeed, most women of my age do.

MARY WORTLEY MONTAGU,
1759

Men are taught to apologize for their weaknesses, women for their strengths.

LOIS WYSE

It is only when a woman surrenders her life to her husband, reveres and worships him, and is willing to serve him, that she becomes really beautiful to him.

MARABEL MORGAN

When a man gets up to speak, people listen then look. When a woman gets up, people *look*; then, if they like what they see, they listen.

PAULINE FREDERICK

First time you buy a house you see how pretty the paint is and buy it. The second time you look to see if the basement has termites. It's the same with men.

LUPE VELEZ

It's not the men in my life that counts—it's the life in my men.

MAE WEST

Index